My Grandmother's COOKBOOK

Traditional Manx Fare and Celtic Customs

COMPILED BY
SUE WOOLLEY

Lily Publications

ISBN: 978-1-907945-07-6

Published by:
Lily Publications Ltd
PO Box 33
Ramsey
Isle of Man
IM99 4LP

www.lilypublications.co.uk

Typeset in ITC Garamond and Lorimer.

Contents

Acknowledgements

I would like to say a few words about two of the photographers whose work is featured in this book and record my gratitude to Manx National Heritage for permission to use these images, many of which have not been published previously.

George Bellett Cowen (1864-1948) was born in Douglas and attended the Douglas School of Art where he was a fellow student of Archibald Knox. He had a studio in Ramsey for many years and took portraits of many well-known personalities of the day. He also made excursions into the countryside carrying heavy photographic equipment - half plate cameras, big wooden tripods and boxes of slides - in his quest to capture the rural way of life before it disappeared. His work in both areas shows outstanding skill and artistry.

William Charles Southward M.L.C., C.P., J.P. (1866-1943) was a near contemporary of G.B. Cowen and belonged to a well-known and respected Sulby family.The Southward family was steeped in Methodism and as well as being a pillar of the local chapel, he composed a number of hymns and sacred songs. As an amateur photographer, he, like Cowen, sought to record the last vestiges of an old way of life and his work is preserved in the Manx Museum Library.

My thanks in producing this book also go to the following:
My family for their encouragement.

Friends who shared recipes and loaned photographs, especially Bev and Del Richardson, Joe Pennington, Margaid, Penny, Mavis, Heidi, Marinda, Janet and Guy.

Staff at the Manx Museum Library for their assistance. The Manx Heritage Foundation for financial assistance.

Introduction

In days gone by, self-sufficiency was a way of life in the rural areas of the Isle of Man, occupying nearly all the daylight hours and involving all members of the household, young and old.

Manx Gaelic was still spoken in the country areas and livelihoods depended on crofting and fishing. 'Priddhas an' herrin' (potatoes and herring) was widely regarded as the national dish.

For centuries, the people relied on the success of the herring season. Herring provided nourishment throughout the year, fresh or kippered in summer, salted or cured in winter.

While the men were at sea in the summer, the women and children took care of the home and carried on the work in the fields. The crofters kept cows, goats, pigs, geese and a few sheep, perhaps the four-horned loaghtyn which is native to the Island and provided soft brown wool which kept the women busy spinning yarn for the weaver.

At the height of summer, when the cow provided plenty of milk, dairying was a full-time occupation for one of the women of the house whose job was to produce butter and cheese for market. Sometimes, ewe's milk was added to assist the turning of the milk for cheese-making. Certain herbs were also used for this purpose.

Every district had a water-mill ready to receive large and

small quantities of grain. Wheat was ground finely for flour; barley was roasted and ground into meal for bread-making or pearled for thickening the broth; oats were ground for oatcakes and rolled for porridge.

Potatoes appeared on the table nearly every day of the year in one form or another, usually accompanied by a herring, a cup of cold butter and plenty of buttermilk to wash it down.

As the days grew shorter, thoughts would turn to the long dark days ahead when fresh food would be scarce. Herrings were hung outside the cottage to dry. A crock was filled to the brim with layers of fish and salt. Geese were killed, quartered and salted - the feathers kept to provide flocking for pillows. The broth pot simmering above the fire was the mainstay, with a little variety provided by a rabbit or hare caught in the fields.

Manx traditional cookery reflects the work and beliefs of the people - it was simple, wholesome fare that made the best use of the available ingredients and very little was wasted.

Thomas Kelly, who wrote about Manx farming in 1812 observed that the diet was 'somewhat coarse'; nevertheless, the people were 'robust, full of energy and capable of work.'

A round three-legged pot was used for cooking porridge, broth and potatoes and herring. It was hung from a chain (*slouree*) over the turf fire which burned slowly and steadily in the big open hearth (*choillagh*). The lid was flat and could hold glowing pieces of turf on top to ensure an even heat. The pot oven was used to bake pies, puddings and even roast a goose at Christmas.

A griddle, a flat circular metal plate could hang from the chain or rest on a metal tripod (*croue*). Straw, bracken (*fearin*), potato stalks and briars were all used under the griddle. Some skill was involved in making soda cake, drop scones and slim cake in this way.

Some cottages had ovens built into a recess beside the fireplace. On baking day, these 'wall ovens' were heated by burning gorse (*bons*) or ling (*heather*) inside until the desired temperature was reached. The fuel would be raked out and the oven brushed out with a goose wing. Soon a batch of *bonnags* and barley cakes would be brought forth.

As it was a lengthy task to prepare the oven, much of the baking was done on an iron griddle over the fire.

It was a hard life and sometimes a struggle to make ends meet, but there was a strong sense of community that endures in the Island to this day. Few of us would care to turn back the clock completely, but we could do worse than follow the folks of old, living simply, close to nature and in harmony with the rhythm of the seasons.

Upper Grange, Narradale

Arran as Caashey

(Bread and Cheese)

If a woman was near to confinement, the people used to remark: 'There'll be bread and cheese in that house in a short time'. This expression stemmed from the fact that it was customary from the birth of the child until its baptism to keep a round tray (dollan) of oatcakes and cheese in the room where the woman was confined. The gossips who came to visit would freely partake of the food, and small pieces of bread and cheese called 'blithe meat' were scattered around the house for the fairies.

When the child was taken to church to be baptised, the woman who carried it also carried some bread and cheese. This was presented to the first person she met - a gesture believed to preserve the child from evil influence.

Oatcakes

(Margaret Christian Cowell's recipe, 1877)

1 breakfast cup of oatmeal
The same of flour
1 tablespoon of sugar
½ teaspoon of bicarbonate of soda
A pinch of salt
½ lb. margarine

Rub all the ingredients well in together and mix to rather a stiff paste with milk and water. Roll out rather thin. Cut in rounds and bake in a moderate oven.

Old Manx Kitchen (Photo: G.B. Cowen) By kind permission of Manx National Heritage

Manx Shortcake

(Traditional)

1 lb. fine oatmeal
½ lb. pound of butter
½ lb. lard (or white vegetable fat)
½ lb. sugar
1 tablespoon baking powder
Pinch of salt

Mix the butter and lard until soft. Mix in the oatmeal and sugar and roll into cakes. Put the dough in dishes rubbed with butter. Place in a hot oven. Cut into squares when baked.

Oatmeal Biscuits

Oat bread steeped in broth and eaten with it was called 'broish'. Anything eaten with bread, such as butter, cheese or milk, was called 'kytshen'.

½ lb. oatmeal
½ lb. flour
1 dessert spoon sugar
2 teaspoons dripping
1 egg
Pinch of baking powder

Mix oatmeal, flour, sugar and baking powder. Melt the dripping and add it to the beaten egg. Add the liquid to the oatmeal mixture and form into a good firm dough. Turn on to a floured board and knead. Roll out thinly, prick with a fork, and cut into rounds. Bake in a very moderate oven for about 20 minutes.

An Old Mill (Photo: G.B. Cowen) By kind permission of Manx National Heritage

Manx Pudding

(Puiddihn Vanninagh)

In country districts especially, people took care that every necessary piece of work which could be done on the Saturday was done, in order to keep the Sabbath free from all but unavoidable labour. Even the water-crocks were filled, so no-one would be required to go to the well or stream on Sunday to fill their buckets.

On a Sabbath morning, or early evening, the neighbours would often gather into the cottage of a friend to hear the Bible read by someone better skilled than the rest in reading.They also attended church or chapel - sometimes the one in the morning and the other in the evening - travelling considerable distances over moor and mountain, in summer and winter.

Fishermen would not go out to fish on a Sunday, and the herring fleet lay in harbour, or at anchor, all the Saturday night and on Sunday.

In the cottages, it was customary to prepare the Sunday meal the previous night. The usual dessert was a batter pudding made of milk and eggs. When rice pudding was introduced into the Island it was called 'sweet porridge with currants in it'. During the rest of the week, the dinner routine on the farms was 'broth, pudding, beef'. The reason, perhaps, was that hungry farm-workers would eat less meat if their appetites were first quelled by helpings of steamed currant pudding.

Country scene

By kind permission of Manx National Heritage

4 oz. plain flour
Pinch of salt
2 eggs
½ pint milk
1 oz. currants

Sieve flour and salt and make a well in the centre.Add the eggs and mix in the flour gradually, slowly adding the milk. Beat well until the mixture is full of bubbles. Stir in the currants. Pour into a greased pudding basin. Cover and steam for about two hours.

Oatmeal Gingerbread

1 lb. flour
½ lb. oatmeal
2 oz. margarine
2 oz. moist brown sugar
1 teaspoon ground ginger
¾ teaspoon baking soda
1 tablespoon syrup
1 tablespoon treacle
1 egg
Buttermilk

Rub the margarine into the flour and add the other dry ingredients. Pour in melted syrup and treacle. Beat in egg and enough buttermilk to make a soft dropping consistency.Turn into a greased tin and bake in a moderate oven for one to one and a half hours.

Manx Cottage 1891 (Photo: J.M. Nicholson) By kind permission of Manx National Heritage

Sollaghan

Shrove Tuesday was called Oie Ynnyd (Eve of the Fast), being the first day before the start of Lent. It was a day for merry-making, when traditional dishes such as Sollaghan and Pancakes were served and fortune-telling games were indulged in.

Sollaghan, served for breakfast, was a mixture of browned oatmeal and gravy, made thus:

'Brown some porridge oatmeal in a pan in front of the fire then add a knob of butter. Skim the broth pot and stir the liquid into the oatmeal until thc mixture sticks together.'

Pancakes were made with buttermilk and a pinch of bicarbonate of soda. Into the batter were thrown a ring and a piece of silver money indicating matrimony or wealth to whoever received the lucky pancakes.

There was an old proverb which warned that such a feast might not always be had:

'At Shrove Tuesday supper if thou belly be full,
before Easter Day thou mayest fast for that'.

It was the day when pupils would lock the teacher out of the school and demand that he or she grant them the rest of the day off from studies, singing 'Holly, Holly, Pancake day: if you don't give us Holly, we'll all run away'.

Although it was traditional to save a sprig of holly from the Christmas decorations to burn under the pan when

Threshing (Photo: W.C. Southward) By kind permission of Manx National Heritage

making pancakes, the holly in the song refers not to the prickly bush, but to a holiday.

Buttered Eggs

Late 18th century recipe

Market Day in Douglas was a great event, with people coming from miles around to do their weekly shopping. Farmers' wives and daughters would be up before dawn, gathering their produce to take and sell. It was a great social occasion - especially for the country folk who rarely visited the towns. The market place would be teeming with people buying and selling eggs, butter, poultry and vegetables and exchanging 'newses'.

Fresh eggs were preserved by wiping the shells clean and coating them with oil, lard or butter, excluding air from penetrating the shells. They were left overnight to dry, then packed in boxes, not touching each other.

12 fresh eggs
Salt
½ lb. butter

Take 12 Eggs, Whites and Yolks, beat them very well and put them in a skillet with a little Salt and pounded Pepper and the Butter. Keep these stirring continually over a very clear Fire, lest you smoke them, till done. Don't do them too hard, take care of burning them. Have broad pieces of White Bread, toasted, layed in your dish. Pour your Egg over it. Serve it hot. If you use nothing but Yolks of the Eggs they are nicer.

Glen Mooar, Michael (Photo G.B. Cowen) By kind permission of Manx National Heritage

Barnee Fryid

(Fried limpets)

The old Manx were very superstitious folk and had many customs and observances attached to Easter-time. It was said: 'He who will drink milk on Good Friday will not find a bird's nest during the year'. It has been suggested that this was meant to deceive the children, because milk was often scarce at that time of year!

In remembrance of the Crucifixion, on no account was any iron to be heated, so the poker and tongs were set aside and a rowan stick was used instead to stir the fire.

A large three-cornered bonnag was baked on the hearthstone to avoid the necessity of handling the griddle over the fire.

It was the practice for the young folk to take an excursion to the beach to collect 'flitters' (limpets) which were eaten for breakfast on Good Friday.

1 quart limpets
Hot butter or lard

Soak the 'flitters' overnight in salt and water, then parboil and take off the shells. Clean them well and fry in hot fat until of a nice brown colour. Serve hot with bread and butter.

Southern Agricultural Show

Salt Herring

Oh, the herrin', boys, The herrin', boys,
The herrin', boys, for me, Red or kippered
Fresh or pickled
The herrin's the King of the Sea
(trad. song)

For centuries, the prosperity of the Isle of Man depended on the success of the herring season and the 'King of the Sea' was the staple diet of the people. In winter, the men would work on their smallholdings, but in summer they would leave the land to reap the harvest of the sea.

Every family had a crock of salted herring for use throughout the year, and sometimes herring would be dried on hooks outside the cottage door.

The reverence with which this fish is regarded is illustrated by the fact that the Deemsters (the Island's supreme judges) take an oath to execute justice as indifferently as 'the herring's backbone doth lie in the midst of the fish'.

Any quantity of fresh herring
Salt
Bay salt
Saltpetre
Brown sugar

Gut the fish and salt them lightly with plain salt. Lay them in a basket and leave them overnight to drain. Wipe each

Old Pete's Cottage, Ramsey

By kind permission of Manx National Heritage

one in a dry cloth to take off all the scales. Pound together equal quantities of saltpetre, bay salt and brown sugar. Place a layer of this in an earthenware crock, then a layer of fish and so on until the crock is full. Spread a thick layer of the salts on top. Cover the crock and leave for a few months before using.

Fatherless Pie

(to be eaten with boiled fish on Good Friday)

2 lb. potatoes
6 oz. butter
1 cupful of milk
1 cupful of water
Pepper and salt
Short Pastry

Slice the potatoes thinly and place in layers, seasoned and dotted with butter, in a casserole dish. Pour over milk and water. Cover with pastry. Bake in a moderate oven.

(The Manx Cookery Book in aid of the Peel Church Spire, 1908)

Lobsterpot maker

By kind permission of Manx National Heritage

Grilled Manx Kippers

The herring season started at the end of May or beginning of June off the west coast and the boats followed the fish southwards round the Island, finishing up at the spawning grounds on the east coast by October.

Traditionally smoked over oak shavings, the herring were cured within hours of being caught. The fish were split, cleaned, washed and put through brine, then hung on frames of tenterhooks and smoked over a slow-burning wood fire for four - six hours. When weighed and packed they were despatched by the morning ferry to the traditional markets of Liverpool, Manchester and Fleetwood.

Kippers are still a popular breakfast dish and can be prepared in a number of ways - fried, baked, poached or grilled. They are a meal in themselves and need no accompaniment other than bread and butter.

One or two kippers per person
Butter

Line the grill rack with foil and heat the grill. Dot the fleshy side of each kipper with butter and grill for about five minutes.

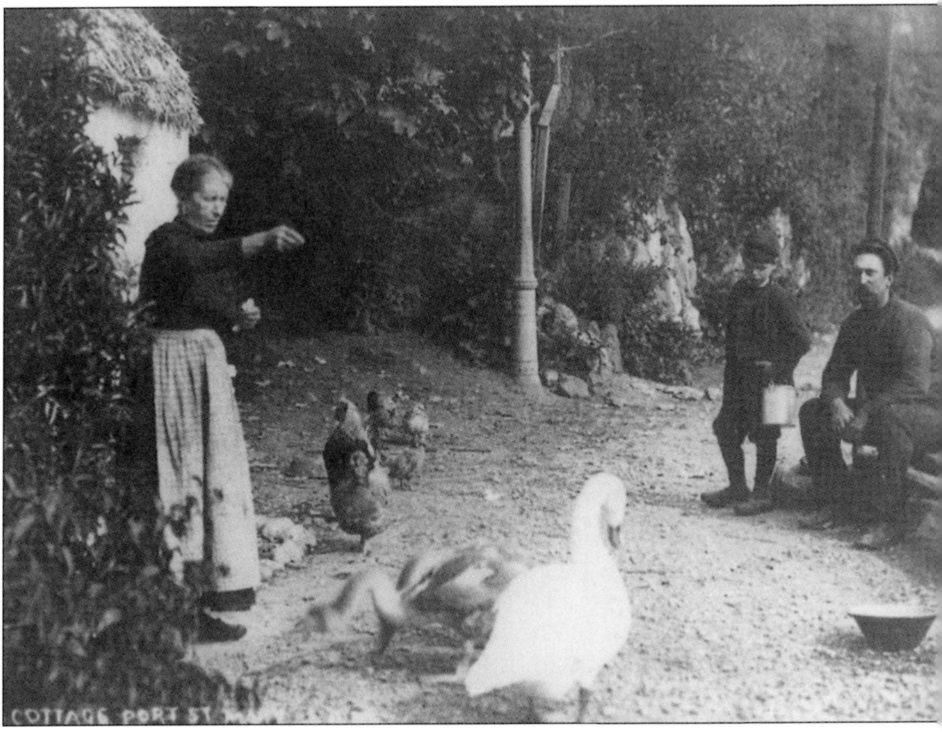

Manx Cottage, Port St Mary

By kind permission of Manx National Heritage

Herring Broth
(Broit Skeddan)

'In the season, we would be coming ashore early every morning for breakfast, carrying about half a hundred of fresh herring with us. We used to go to a public house for breakfast, and the woman there would take the herrings from us and scrape them as clean as clean, and then she would boil a potful for us. When they were done, we would shake the herring from the bone into little brown dishes... We would fill them up with the herring broth, supping it with the herrings. Some of us, to make it more tasty, would sometimes put a scallion in the broth. We would have our own bread and butter to eat with us. Afterwards some would, maybe, have a pint or two of 'jough' and sometimes we would carry a jar of it on board with us.'
* Roeder, C (ed.) (1904) Manx Notes and Queries, part of a Peel fisherman's account of life in the 1800's. Douglas Isle of Man : Broadbent, Examiner Office.

10 fresh herring
Shallots or chives
Pepper and salt

Clean and scrape the herrings well, removing heads and tails. Place in a pot with the shallots, finely chopped, add salt and pepper to taste. Add one quart of cold water. Bring to the boil and simmer for 15 minutes. Serve the herrings in the broth, removing the bones.
(Caesar Cashin, Peel).

Manx Fishermen in Shetland

By kind permission of Manx National Heritage

Dalby Sandwich

(Mr J. Moore, Patrick)

'Take a piece of barley cake and spread it over with fresh butter, add a layer of potatoes, bruised, then a coating of salt herring nicely picked and free of bones; upon this spread another layer of potatoes and cover with barley cake and butter. A seasoning of pepper is an improvement.'

This was said to be a good 'braghtyn' to put in your pocket when you are going on a journey.

Fried Herring Roes

½ lb. herring roes or melts (soft roes)
Seasoned flour
1 ½ oz. butter

Dip roes in the seasoned flour and gently fry in the butter for about eight minutes.

Herring fleet in Peel

By kind permission of Manx National Heritage

Priddhas An' Herrin'

I'm a native of Peel
And I think for a meal
That there's nuthin' like priddhas an' herrin'.
I was rared on the quay
An' I followed the say
An' it's mighty good fishin' I'm gerrin'
(Traditional song)

Two herrings per person
Potatoes
Raw onion

This is probably the most renowned of all Manx dishes, and one of the simplest to prepare. Use salt herring which have been soaked in fresh water overnight. Scrub the potatoes, put them in a large saucepan and barely cover with water. When the potatoes are just over half cooked, lay the herring on top. When both are cooked, carefully lift out the herring, drain the potatoes and serve with slices of raw onion and knobs of butter. This dish is traditionally served with plenty of buttermilk to drink.

James 'Jim' Cottier, coxswain of the Ramsey lifeboat 1890-1910
(Photo: G.B. Cowen)

By kind permission of Manx National Heritage

Potted Herring

In Peel, as in all fishing communities, superstitions abounded. Signs and omens were never ignored and some of the old rituals believed to court a successful season still survive. An old saying goes: 'If custom will not get custom, custom will weep'.

The first herring of the season taken out of the nets was always put aside and boiled whole, to mark it from the others which would have the heads and tails cut off. When the fish were cooked, every man on board had to come and take a pick of the first herring. This was to symbolise 'share and share alike' throughout the season. The cook would always throw a few fish over boat, for luck, to the merman (Yn Dooiney-Marrey) for his breakfast.

2 herring per person
Salt
Vinegar and water
1 teaspoon of pickling spice
2 or 3 bay leaves

Scrape the scales from the fresh herring and clean them, cutting off the heads. Lay them in an oven-proof dish, cover with vinegar and water, add pickling spice, salt and bay leaves. Cover the dish, bring to the boil, then simmer in a moderate oven until the bones are cooked right through. Serve cold.

Peel fisherman William Quirk with grandson Allan McMeiken

Barleymeal-Potato Bonnags

'Every Monday morning we would carry the week's grub from home with us in a wallet slung round our necks – something after the shape of a shepherd's purse. We would have about a pound of butter in a round wooden screw-capped box. Some would take oatcakes made in very thick quarters, and baked as hard as hard over the fire. My mother would be giving me little bonnags of barleymeal and potatoes kneaded well together, baked in a pot-oven'.

Roeder, C. (ed.) (1904) Manx Notes and Queries : part of a Peel fisherman's account of life in the 1800's. Douglas, Isle of Man : Broadbent, Examiner Office.

4 oz. freshly mashed potatoes
6 oz. barley flour
1 ½ oz. melted butter
1 ½ teaspoons baking powder
Pinch of salt
Milk to mix

Mix together the flour, salt and baking powder. Rub in the fat very thoroughly. Add the potatoes and mix in lightly. Knead to a soft dough with the cold milk. Turn on to a floured board, roll or pat out half an inch thick. Cut into rounds and place on a greased baking sheet. Bake in a hot oven for about 15 minutes.

Ramsey harbour

Furmity

A warming breakfast dish

When the way of life for most Manx people was crofting and fishing, the main crops were barley and oats. Wheat did not become a common commodity until the early 1800s.

There were water mills in use all over the Island for hundreds of years, and large and small amounts of grain were taken to them to be ground. Barley was ground into meal for baking or was pearled for broth, while oats were ground coarsely for porridge, and finely for bread, oatcakes and biscuits. The larger, less accessible farms had their own horse-driven grinding mills.

Porridge of one kind or another was frequently served at meal time. Thomas Kelly, writing in the 1850s, said flour porridge was common in the north, as considerably more wheat was grown there than in any other part of the Island.

'And when lads or maidens enjoyed a breakfast or supper of this porridge they were equal to any necessary requirement following....'

Shelled barley
A little flour
Milk
Raisins (optional)

Take some shelled barley and boil it in water for about an hour. Then stir a little flour in some cold milk and add the liquid to the barley pot. Stir well and bring to the boil. Add some raisins if desired. Simmer until thickened. Furmity is better if made the night before.

Old Mill pond (Photo: G.B. Cowen) By kind permission of Manx National Heritage

Barleymeal Bonnag

(Bonnag Arran Oarn)

Barley was dried on a hot hearth or stone heated over a turf fire and then ground in a quern (handmill) or a millstone made of granite. But in 1647, Lord Derby, whose family owned the Island, ordered the destruction of all handmills so that the people would be forced to use the Lord's mills.

¾ lb. barleymeal
¼ lb. plain flour
2 oz. lard or margarine
1 small teaspoon baking powder
1 small teaspoon cream of tartar
1 small teaspoon salt
½ pint buttermilk (approx.)

Put the barleymeal, flour and salt in a bowl and rub in the fat. Mix the baking powder and cream of tartar with the buttermilk. Add the liquid to the dry ingredients and mix to a soft dough. Shape into two or three loaves and bake in a moderate oven for an hour. To make sweet loaves, add currants to the mixture and sprinkle the loaves with sugar.

Spinning yarn

By kind permission of Manx National Heritage

Barley Bread

An Old Manx Dish

The traditional way of making barley bread was to mix the finely ground meal with water into a dough which was kneaded into thin, round cakes. The cakes, which were clapped flat between the hands, were known as 'berreens'.

Barley flour is particularly tasty if pan-roasted before making it into a dough. This gives the bread a moist, cake-like consistency.

Pott mie dy vainney bruie
Lesh crie braew dy veinn er,
Lesh berreen dy arran oarn
Lesh cheeid dty vass dy ceym er.

A good pot of boiling milk
With a brave shake of meal on it
And a cake of barley bread
With butter on it as thick as your hand

Milking time

By kind permission of Manx National Heritage

Cowree

A recipe filched from the L'il People

After the oats were ground at the mill, the husks would also be returned and were used to make 'cowree', a thick gruel which was the traditional dish left by the hearth at night for the fairies or 'L'il people' as the Manx folk called them.

Cowree was also the food taken up the mountain for sustenance on a turf-cutting day, such as that described by Canon John Quine in his book 'The Captain of the Parish' (1897):

'To be first on the ground meant the choice of the best cuttings, and long before dawn the whole country was up and away to be on the spot by sunrise. It was a jollification of hard work and of feasting - a bivouac on the brown mountain waste of hundreds of country carts and thousands of folk, fires blazing, kettles steaming, frying pans hissing, round-bottomed pots bubbling, universal hailings, greetings, laughter, courtings - for women, girls and children are all there by prerogative right...

'The folk from the distant northern plain camp all night on the mountainside, each family with a cartload of bedding and a sailcloth rigged over the carts. These night campers are the envy of all. The song is sung and the tale told with pipes and stone jars of ale around the fire; and the old men are to the fore recounting the doings that went on in the past days'.

Ford at Cornaa village, Maughold

To make cowree, steep the husks of a bushel of oats with a handful or two of fine oatmeal for nine days, in sufficient water to cover. When it has fermented and become bitter, run the water through a sieve to remove the husks. Now fill the biggest pot you have in the house with the liquid. Stir with a pot stick all the time it is on the fire until it becomes thick and solid. When it is quite cold, boil it with milk and serve.

The cloudy water in which the husks and oatmeal had been steeped was sometimes drunk without being boiled, and this was called 'sooslagh' - a drink with body in it.

Rich Fruit Bonnag

1 lb. self raising flour
6 oz. margarine
8 oz. demerara sugar
½ pint milk and water
½ lb. dried fruit (sultanas and currants)
2 teaspoons mixed spice
½ teaspoon salt

Rub the margarine into the flour. Add the sugar and all dry ingredients. Stir in the milk and water to form a dough. Place in two 1 lb. loaf tins (lined). Bake in the centre of a moderate oven for 1¼ hours.

At the turbary (cutting turf)
(Photo: W.C. Southward)

By kind permission of Manx National Heritage

Binjean
(Curds and Whey)

Butter was made on the farm by blowing the cream of each day's milk into the 'bithag crock'. When the cream ripened, it was transferred to the churn and beaten until the butter separated from the buttermilk. If a black cat wandered into the dairy at churning time it was considered unlucky, although at other times the opposite view was held. New milk would never brought out of doors without a drop of water in it - to keep the fairies away; and at every churning time, a small bit of butter was stuck on the wall for them. Butter was also used for the healing of cuts and bruises and thick cream was used to soften wounds and as a treatment for sunburn.

1 pint milk
1 teaspoon rennet

Made in the summer when there was plenty of milk, 'binjean' (pronounced 'pinjane') was a very popular dessert, using milk warm from the cow. If using cold milk, heat it gently to blood temperature. Add one teaspoon of rennet to the warm milk and allow it to cool and set (about half an hour).

'Binjean' was usually eaten plain, just sprinkled with sugar.

Old lady with spinning wheel

By kind permission of Manx National Heritage

Dressed Crab

A great occupation with the children was digging in the sand at the edge of the tide for 'gibbins' (sand eels). These would be taken home and fried for tea, or sold by the quart. Fish- sellers used to travel from the fishing ports to all the country areas in spring-carts, offering 40 or 50 fresh herring for a shilling, or a large cod for two shillings.

Crabs are plentiful in the shallow pools among the rocks when the tide is out. In season from April to June, crabmeat has a delicate flavour. Bread rolls filled with dressed crab are a speciality at some of the local hostelries.

1 or 2 crabs (ready cooked)
Mayonnaise
½ – 1 oz. fresh breadcrumbs
Salt, pepper, mustard

Crabs are usually sold ready-cooked. To prepare a crab, remove the flesh from the shell and claws, discarding the small stomach sac and the greyish-brown flesh. Put the creamy-brown and white flesh in a bowl and mix together with some mayonnaise, breadcrumbs and seasonings.

Shoeing the horse (Photo: W.C. Southward) By kind permission of Manx National Heritage

Tanrogans

One of the most popular shellfish caught in local waters is the scallop, called 'tanrogan' in the Isle of Man. 'Tanrogan' was originally the name given to the scallop shell when it was filled with cod oil to provide a lamp for the fishermen.A rush, which quickly soaked up the oil, was used for the wick.

Small scallops, 'queenies' have become increasingly popular in recent years and are exported in large quantities all over the world.They can be lightly fried in oil and butter or bacon fat, stewed in wine or milk, or deep fried in batter.There are between eight and 12 scallops to the 1lb. compared with 40- 80 queenies.The following is a modern recipe for baked tanrogans with a cheese sauce:

8 scallops
¼ pint fish stock
I small onion, quartered
Salt and pepper
1 bay leaf

Remove scallops from their shells and clean, but do not remove the coral tip. Place in an oven-proof dish with the stock, onion, seasoning and bay leaf. Cover and cook gently in a moderate oven for about 10 minutes. Lift out the scallops and replace them in their shells and reserve the liquor to make the sauce.

Tholtan, Cornaa valley

Cheese Sauce

1 oz. butter
1 oz. flour
½ pint milk/liquor
2 oz. Cheddar cheese
2 tablespoons cream

Melt the butter, stir in the flour and cook over a low heat for one minute. Remove from heat, add milk/ liquor, stirring thoroughly to blend. Bring to the boil, lower heat and stir until thickened. Remove from heat and beat in cream and half the grated cheese. Pour a little of the sauce into each scallop shell, sprinkle with the rest of the grated cheese and brown under the grill. Serve with piped mashed potatoes.

Groosniuys

'Groosniuys' (pronounced 'crusnous') was a custard-like pudding made with milk from the second milking after a cow had calved.The milk, mixed with a little salt and sugar, was placed in a double-boiler to prevent curdling, and sprinkled with nutmeg. It was left to cook very slowly until firm and golden brown.

Scallop shells

By kind permission of Manx National Heritage

Queenies in Batter with Tartare Sauce

½ lb. queenies
Seasoned flour

The Batter

3oz. plain flour
1oz. dried white breadcrumbs
1 tablespoon vegetable oil
1 egg
¼ pint milk

Poach the queenies in water until tender, drain and coat with the seasoned flour. Prepare the batter by adding the beaten egg to the sifted flour and breadcrumbs and gradually adding the milk and oil. Dip the queenies into the batter using a skewer. Fry in deep oil, a few at a time, for about three minutes or until golden brown. Drain on kitchen paper and sprinkle with salt. Serve at once with tartare sauce.

Tartare Sauce

4 spring onions
2 teaspoons parsley
1 tablespoon capers or gherkins
A little mayonnaise
2 teaspoons lemon juice

Mince the spring onions, parsley, capers and gherkins. Beat the mayonnaise until creamy. Mix all the ingredients together, adding lemon juice, to taste.

Bee hives

By kind permission of Manx National Heritage

Honey Fudge

Every household had at least one or two hives of bees to keep the family supplied with honey. It was used just as we use sugar today. Sometimes, the hives were taken up the mountain to allow the bees to feed on the heather. Bees also love fuchsia - maybe that is why so much grew around the old cottages.

There used to be a great many fairs throughout the year, but the longest surviving one is Tynwald Fair, the Manx national day, held in the village of St John's on July 5th (Old Midsummer Day). This is the day the Acts of Tynwald (the Manx parliament) are promulgated and it is both a solemn and a lively affair. In days gone by, the fairground was dotted with shies and stalls, bands, and groups of dancers in national costume. It is still a great place to meet friends you may not have seen since the previous Fair Day.

One of the most popular sweetmeats on sale is home-made fudge:

1 lb. sugar
2 oz. plain chocolate
¼ teaspoon salt
1 cup evaporated milk
3 tablespoons honey
2 tablespoons butter

Boil the sugar, chocolate, salt and milk for five minutes. Add the honey and cook to a soft-ball stage (240 degrees F). Remove from heat and add the butter. Let stand until lukewarm, then beat until creamy and pour into a buttered tray. Cut when firm.

Ramsey harbour

Potato Cakes

Potatoes became the staple diet at the beginning of the 19th century when they superseded barley and oats. According to Thomas Quayle writing in 1812 about Manx agriculture, potatoes appeared 'on the table of all ranks of people nearly every day in the year.' They were cooked in their jackets and eaten with salt herring, mashed and made into potato cakes, and added to stews and hot-pots.

The common name for mashed potatoes was 'tittlewhack' - derived from the sound made by the wooden pestle used to mash big tubs of potatoes. While jacket potatoes were put on the table in a long wooden tray, 'tittlewhack' was served in a dish along with a cup of cold butter.

When the first new potato of the season was eaten, it was believed to be lucky to make a wish, as it was sure to be granted.

½ lb. mashed potatoes
1 oz. butter
Flour
1 teaspoon sugar

Rub the butter into the potatoes, add as much flour as will make a moderately stiff paste. Add sugar to taste. Roll out as thin as a pancake. Cut with a saucer. Bake on a moderately hot griddle. Have ready a hot plate and butter as you bake them and serve hot.

Peel Primitive Methodist outing

Bonnag

8 oz. plain flour
1 - 2 oz. butter or margarine
Pinch of salt
1 cup of buttermilk
1 teaspoon bicarbonate of soda
1 teaspoon cream of tartar

Sift the flour and salt into a bowl and rub in the fat. Mix together the buttermilk, bicarbonate of soda and cream of tartar. Gradually add the liquid to the dry ingredients and mix with a fork to make a soft dough. Turn onto a floured board and knead the dough lightly until smooth. Shape into a round and place on a greased baking tray. Mark into sections and brush the top with milk. Bake in a moderate oven for 30- 40 minutes until well-risen and golden brown.

Griddle Cakes

1lb flour
½ tspn salt
Baking soda to cover a shilling
Buttermilk to mix

Mix together the flour and baking soda, rub in the salt and gradually work the milk in with the hands. Roll out to thin round cakes (about half an inch) and bake on a hot greased griddle over the fire until lightly browned on both sides. Griddle cakes can be eaten hot or cold, and buttered.

'Master Frank' at Ramsey harbour

Manx Broth

'I don't know how to make it, but I know when it is good!' - A.H. Laughton, former High Bailiff of Peel
The traditional dish served at a Manx wedding feast was broth, which was eaten from wooden bowls known as 'piggins' and supped with mussel shells called 'sligs'. The guests travelled to church on horseback and when the ceremony was over they would gallop as fast as they could to the bride's house. The first person to reach the house tried to catch a slipper from the bride's foot, and small pieces of wedding cake were scatted over her head as she was going inside. All the friends and relatives brought something towards the feast and there would be a lavish spread of fowls and cold meats to follow the broth.

A barrel of ale was put on top of the hedge outside the house for people who were not at the wedding, and inside there would be plenty of 'jough' (ale) and wine.

Piece of shin beef
Marrow bone
Salt
2oz pearl barley
Diced vegetables
Sprig of thyme
Parsley

Boil shin and bone together with a good pinch of salt. Keep topping up the water and when the meat is cooked take it out. (The meat can be served cold as a separate meal).

Old lady, Cornaa village

By kind permission of Manx National Heritage

Put the stock on the heat again with the barley which has been soaked overnight. Let the liquid simmer until the barley is cooked, stirring occasionally to prevent it from sticking. Then add the diced vegetables - potatoes, turnip, carrot, parsnip, leeks, beans, cabbage, celery etc. Add the thyme and parsley and keep the broth simmering until the vegetables are cooked through. Serve with suet dumplings.

Pea Soup

(Mrs Wm. Mylrea, St Germain's Place, Peel†)

1 lb dried whole peas
3 quarts water
2 onions
1 small turnip
2 lbs. potatoes
1 ½ lb. beef
1 lb. bacon
Pepper and salt to taste

Soak peas overnight in cold water and then drain off the water. Put all the ingredients, except potatoes and onions, into a pan and boil for one and a half hours. Then add the chopped onions and sliced potatoes and simmer gently until the potatoes are cooked.

†From The Manx Cookery Book in aid of Peel Church Spire Re-building Fund, 1908.

The stream at Ballaglass (Photo G.B. Cowen) By kind permission of Manx National Heritage

Michaelmas Goose

Traditionally, roast goose was eaten on Michaelmas Day (September 29).The bird was stuffed with sage and onion stuffing and served with boiled potatoes, mustard and apple sauce. It was usually a young bird and was sometimes called 'Green Goose'.

Stuff the prepared bird with sage and onion stuffing. Put some fat from the inside of the goose over the breast and roast it in a baking tin in a moderate oven for half an hour, then add one cup of hot water to the fat. Baste the bird every 20 minutes and cook until tender, allowing 20 - 25 minutes to the pound. Use the giblets to make stock for the gravy.

Apple Sauce

2 lb. cooking apples
1 - 2 oz. butter or margarine
Sugar, if desired

Peel, core and slice the apples and stew to a pulp in a covered pan. Beat until smooth and add the butter or margarine. If the apples are too tart, add a little sugar.

The Gleaners

Mheillea Pie

There was always great rejoicing when the last of the corn was reaped at harvest time and it was usual for the farmer to provide a supper for all the workers. The end of the reaping was known as the Mheillea.

When the last sheaf was cut, it was made into a garland with wildflowers and bound with a ribbon. This garland, known as 'The Maiden', was carried by one of the women reapers to the highest part of the field, amid the cheers of the other workers. A small sheaf taken from 'The Maiden' was preserved until the following harvest and was called the 'Harvest Doll'.

The workers put on their best clothes to attend the harvest supper and after the meal there was singing and dancing to the music of a fiddler until the early hours. The atmosphere and colour of one of these occasions was recalled in a poem by a man named Hudson which was published in the Manx Sun. It intimates that the farmer's wife was expected to entertain on a grand scale:

'That broth was broth now: cooks take a hint, A
hundred gallons, there'd be no less:
Firm beef and mutton and barley no stint, And a
ham or two all of the bes'.
*Apple dumplings like *perkhans went rollin' about,*
Playin' hide and go seek with the hams;
While a shower of barley and greens showed out,
Setting hungry f 'las rubbin' their palms.'

* porpoises

Manx cottage

By kind permission of Manx National Heritage

A dish popularly served at the supper was herring pie. It was usually made with potatoes, but the following version was found in a late 18th century cookery book.

6 fresh herring
½ teaspoon mace
Salt and pepper
3 large cooking apples
2 onions
A little butter

Line a large oven-proof dish with pastry. Scale, gut and clean the herring, removing heads, fins and tails. Season the fish with the mace, salt and pepper. Put a little butter in the bottom of the pie dish, and then a row of herring. Pare the apples and place thin slices over the fish. Slice the onions and lay on top of the apple. Put a little butter on top and pour on a quarter of a cup of water. Cover with pastry and bake in a moderate oven for 30 - 40 minutes.

Hasty Pudding

1 pt milk
1 tblspn plain flour
1 tblspn fine or medium oatmeal
Pinch of salt

Mix the dry ingredients with a quarter of the milk to make a sloppy paste. Bring the remainder of the milk to the boil and stir in the paste. Keep stirring as you cook until the mixture thickens. Serve with cream and honey.

Cornmill, Malew (Photo G.B. Cowen)

Nettle Beer

Apart from buttermilk, the most popular beverage was ale and most farmers brewed their own. At one time, there was a brewing-house in every parish. In 1650, the price of beer and ale was 2d per quart. Hot ale, flavoured with ginger, pepper and other spices was traditionally drank at the nearest inn after the Oie'll Verrey (eve of St Mary's Feast) service on Christmas Eve. Warm ale and eggs were once used to make a syllabub, but this recipe seems to have been lost as the years have passed.

1 lb. or more of nettles and dandelion leaves
1 lb. sugar
1 oz. dried yeast
2 gallons water
Piece of toast

Boil the nettles and dandelion leaves in the water. Strain the liquid into a crock. Dissolve the sugar in the liquid. Place the yeast on a piece of cold toast and float the toast on the liquid. Leave to 'work' for three to four hours. Remove toast and yeast and bottle the liquid. Leave for at least three days.

Stormy seas at Ramsey

Blackberry Wine

An old recipe which is easy to follow, for a liqueur-type wine, especially good at Christmas.

Put 3 lb. of blackberries in a stone jar with three dessertspoons of sugar. Leave for three weeks, stirring every day. Strain through a muslin bag and add one pound of sugar to every pint of juice. Pour into bottles and add a dessert spoonful of brandy to each bottle. Cork and leave for a few weeks.

Home-made Ginger Beer

(Margaret Christian Cowell, 1878)

Take two lemons. Remove the peel. Slice the lemons and put in a vessel with the peel, 1 oz. cream of tartar and 3 lb. sugar. Boil 1 oz. crushed ginger in three gallons of water and pour over the other ingredients. Allow the mixture to stand until cool. Add 2 tablespoons of yeast. Let it stand 14 - 16 hours. Strain into bottles. Cork tightly.

Pulling 'bent' for thatching at the Ayres By kind permission of Manx National Heritage

Herb Beer

The herb Vervain, known as 'Vervine' or 'Yn Lhus' ('the herb') has always been credited with magical properties by the Manx people. A tall plant with spiky leaves and small mauve flowers, it has been said to cure eye, throat and respiratory diseases, liver complaints and feverish conditions. When the fishing industry ran up against hard times, a 'fairy Doctor' was sometimes call in. One of his remedies was to take a bunch of Vervain, boil it in a little water in a boat's cooking pot and sprinkle the water on each net as it was cast. This was sure to bring up the nets brimful of herring. In the same belief, Vervain was sometimes put in the buoys which floated the nets.

Take one handful each of Vervain, Nettles, Yarrow, Wild Carrot, St John's Wort, Centaury, Marsh Mallow, and either Horehound or Hops. Boil together in two gallons of water for half an hour. Strain off the liquid and add to it one pound of sugar. Let it stand until lukewarm. Then add two ounces of fresh yeast or one ounce of dried yeast, cover and let the mixture 'work'. Skim and bottle. Leave for three days or more.

Mowing the corn

By kind permission of Manx National Heritage

Elderflower Wine

The uplands of the Island are scattered with the ruins of former prosperous farms, sometimes now no more than a heap of stones. These 'tholtans' were once the homes of a hard-working people who depended on the land for a living and were as self-sufficient as was possible.

In many respects, the hill folk were better off than the lowlanders: they had plenty of good spring water, while the inhabitants of some villages had to share a common well, and with horses and traps for transport they were no more cut off than some lowland farms. They grew crops to feed the animals and provide the household with flour and vegetables, kept hens or geese for eggs, bees for honey and a cow for milk. They had plenty of fuel in the form of peat. They brewed their own ale and wines from cultivated and wild produce and made preserves from the harvest of the hedgerows. By the beginning of last century, families were leaving the hills, and many men found work on the railways. They not only left their homes, they also left a way of life behind them.

In the garden of almost every old Manx cottage can be seen an Elder tree (tramman). This tree was used as a charm for protecting houses and gardens from the influence of sorcery and witchcraft. Its leaves, like those of the Rowan (cuirn), were picked on May Eve and fixed to doors and windows to protect the household from evil influence.

St. John's Mart

4 – 6 Elder flowers in full bloom
2 tablespoons white wine vinegar
Juice of 1 lemon
1 ½ lb. sugar
1 gallon cold water

Put all the ingredients into a large container and leave for 24 hours. Sieve, bottle and leave for about a fortnight.

Beef Tea

From a recipe dated February 18th, 1863

Beef tea makes a good nourishing drink, especially for invalids.

½ lb. lean beef
¾ pint water
Pinch of salt

Shred the meat and remove all the fat. Pour the water into a jar and add the salt. Place the meat in the water and let it stand for an hour if possible. Then put the jar into a pan of boiling water and keep the water bubbling for two hours. Remove the jar from the pan. Strain the beef liquid to remove remaining fat. Before serving, add more salt if necessary.

Thatched Manx cottage

Vegetable Marrow Jam

4 lb. vegetable marrow (when peeled)
4 lb sugar
1 lb. preserved ginger
1 teaspoon lemon essence
2 oz. salt

Remove seeds from the marrow and dice it. Sprinkle the marrow with the salt and leave overnight. Next day, put all the ingredients in a pan and boil gently until the marrow is clear. The jam is cooked when a little placed on a cold plate sets. Pour into warm, dry jars and seal at once.

Rosehip Jelly

Gather the hips when red and well-ripened. Wash and drain, then boil in enough water to barely cover until the flesh is very soft. Put in a muslin bag and allow to drain overnight. Use 1 lb. sugar to each pint of liquid and boil together until setting point is reached, then pot in the usual way.

Hop tu Naa turnip lantern

Dumb Cake (Soddag Valloo)

The ancient festival of All Hallowe'en was held on November 11th - the last night of the Celtic year. It was known as Hollantide Eve or 'Hop-tu-Naa' - a name believed to have the same origin as the Scottish Hogmanay.Youths went from house to house knocking on all the doors with cabbages on sticks and singing a traditional song until they were given potatoes, herring, or bonnags. One version of the song went like this:

Hop-tu-Naa – put in the pot;
Hop-tu-Naa – scald me trot
Hop-tu-Naa – I met an old woman;
Hop-tu-Naa – she was baking bonnags
Hop-tu-Naa – I asked for a bit;
Hop-tu-Naa – she gave me a bit,
as big as my big toe.
Hop-tu-Naa – she dipped it in milk,
Hop-tu-Naa – she wrapped it in silk
Hop-tu-Naa, Tra-la-laa
Jinny the Witch flew over the house
To catch a stick to lather the mouse
Hop-tu-Naa, Tra-la-laa
If you don't give us something
We'll run away with the light of the moon....

The traditional supper consisted of potatoes, parsnips and fish mashed together with butter. Left-overs were not removed from the table in case the fairies were hungry, and crocks of fresh water were put out for them.

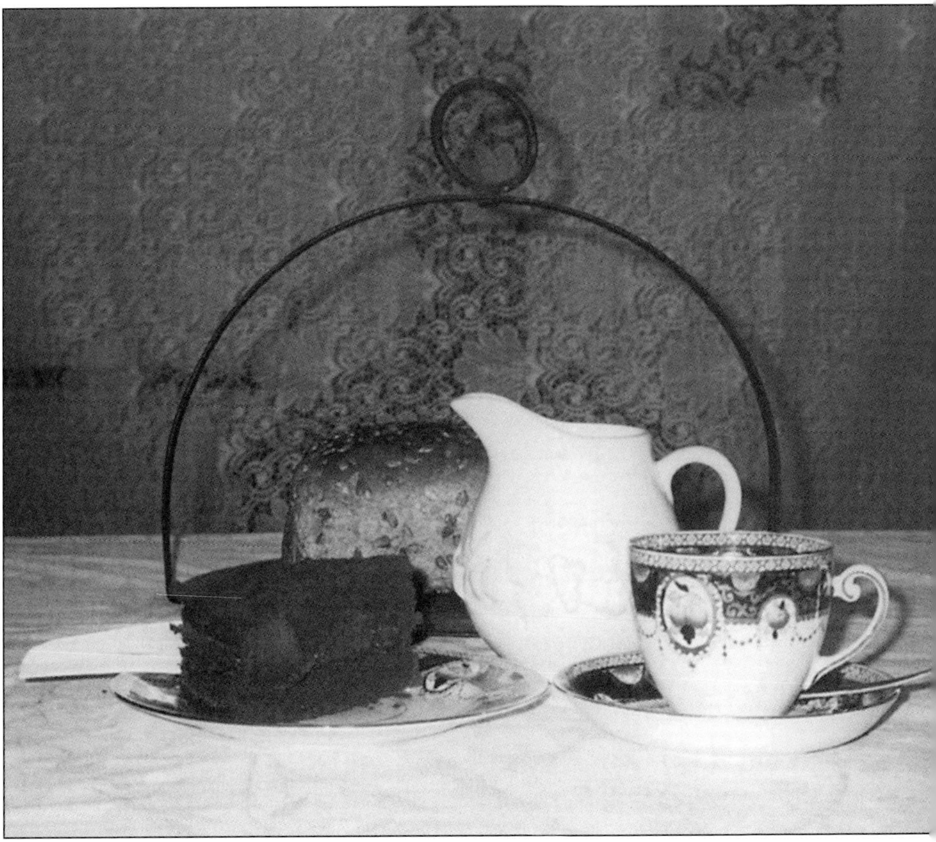

Time for 'Tay'

Dumb Cake (Soddag Valloo) was baked and eaten in silence by young women on Hollantide Eve. It was made from flour and water, without leaven, and baked over the hot turf ashes. A piece was to be eaten while walking backwards towards the bed. Her future husband was supposed to appear in her dreams that night.

Another method of divination was for the young woman to take a salt herring out of pickle, roast it in the embers, eat it all up - head, tail and bones - without speaking and retire to bed in silence, walking often backwards. If she dreamt of a man giving her a drink, he was supposed to be a representation of her future husband.

Nowadays, Hop-tu-Naa is celebrated on October 31st and the children still carry turnip lanterns from house to house.

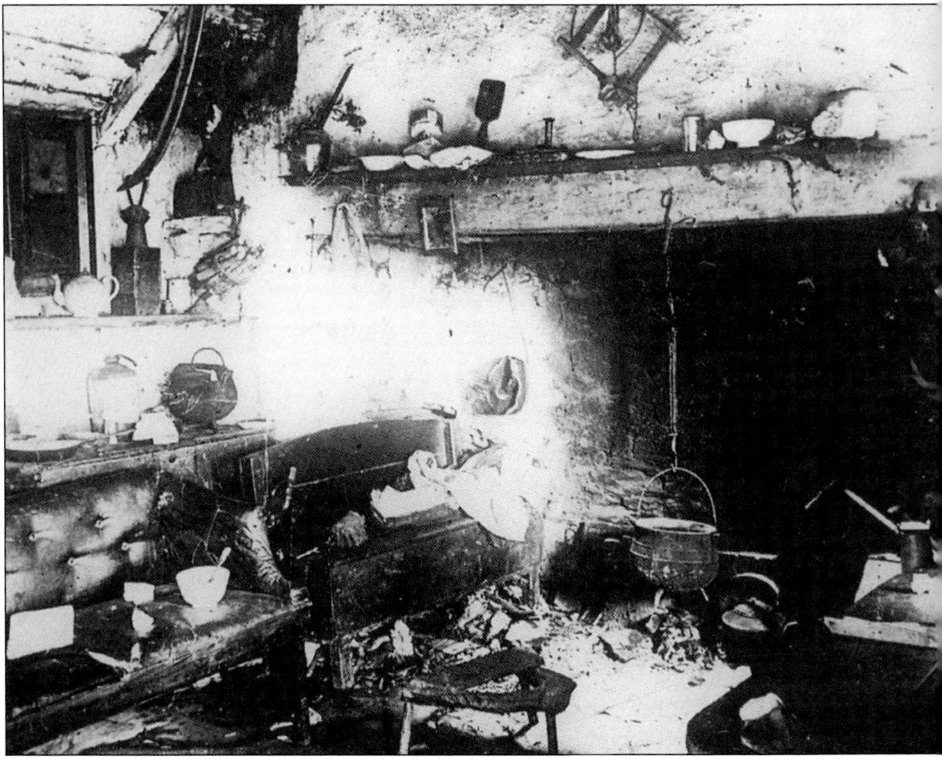

Cottage kitchen (Photo: W.C. Southward) By kind permission of Manx National Heritage

Hollantide Fairings

According to the old calendar, November 12th was the start of the new year and the general day for letting lands, payment of rent and for farm workers to take up their places for the year. Up to about 75 years ago, Hollantide Fairs were held in various parts of the Isle of Man and there would always be stalls selling gingerbread 'fairings'.

3 oz. margarine or butter
2 tablespoons golden syrup
2 oz. sugar
6 oz. flour
1 ½ teaspoons ground ginger
½ teaspoon mixed spice
½ teaspoon bicarbonate of soda
A little water

Melt the fat, syrup and sugar together in a saucepan over a low heat. Sieve the flour and spices into a bowl. Dissolve the bicarbonate of soda in a little water and add to the ingredients in the saucepan, then mix in with the dry ingredients to form a dough. Cover the bowl and leave for at least one hour. Roll out thinly and cut into fancy shapes (traditionally men on horseback) using a cutter or cardboard pattern. Bake in a moderate oven for about 15 minutes. When the biscuits are cold, decorate them with icing sugar, lemon peel and currants.

Ballasalla Mart - Arthur Dick, auctioneer; Jimmy Martin, secretary

Traditional Hollantide Eve Supper Dish

Soak salt bollan* overnight and boil until tender. Serve with mashed potatoes and parsnips.

* wrasse

Slim Cake

1 lb. flour
4 oz. fat
1 egg
3 oz. sugar
2 oz. currants
⅓ pint milk

Sift flour into a bowl and rub in fat. Add beaten egg, sugar and currants and gradually stir in milk to make a soft, but not sticky dough. Roll out the dough very thinly and cut into oblongs, measuring three inches by four inches. Bake on a griddle or frying pan, turning after a few minutes, until cooked.

Manx cat

Gingerbread

'My hec', what a wonderful scorf we hed,
jellies an' cheese an' ham,
Gingerbread, crackers an' currant loaf,
tater cakes, bonnags an' jam....
For 'atin' cakes an' drinkin tay,
theers none can bate the Manx;
It's a gif', that's what I'm thinkin',
for which we should give thanks.'

(From 'A Manx Tay Party and Concert' by Charles Craine).

1 lb. plain flour
8 oz. soft brown sugar
6 oz. lard or white vegetable fat
6 oz. block margarine
1 cup milk
½ lb. golden syrup
¼ lb. treacle pinch of salt
4 - 5 teaspoons ground ginger
2 eggs
2 teaspoons bicarbonate of soda
1 cup boiling water

Sift the flour and ginger into a large bowl and add the sugar and salt. Melt the lard, margarine and syrup in a pan over a low heat. Add to the flour mixture and stir well. Then add the beaten egg and milk. Lastly, dissolve the bicarbonate of soda in a cup of boiling water (it should be frothy) and add to the mixture, beating well. Pour into a greased and lined square roasting tin and bake on the middle shelf of a low oven for 2 - 2 ½ hours.

Country scene (Photo: W.C. Southward) By kind permission of Manx National Heritage

Fruit Tea Bread

Until the beginning of the 20th century, tea was a scarce commodity and was saved for special occasions. It is on record that when tea was first introduced into the Island, some of the less sophisticated families boiled up the leaves and ate them with butter, while the water was thrown away!

1 lb. flour
1 teaspoon baking powder
8 oz. brown sugar
1 cup warm, milkless tea
1 egg
2 tablespoons marmalade
1 teaspoon mixed spice
8 oz. mixed dried fruit

Steep the fruit and sugar in the tea overnight. Next day, stir in the beaten egg, marmalade, spice and flour. Line a cake or loaf tin with grease-proof paper and cook in a moderate oven for 1¾ hours. Leave to cool before slicing and serve buttered.

Griddle with soda cake

Soda Cake

Miss Rebena Gelling's recipe dated March 30th, 1896

The Manx housewife rarely used yeast in her baking. Instead, equal parts of bicarbonate of soda and cream of tartar were blended together with buttermilk to produce a raising agent which was then mixed with the dry ingredients. On the crofts, the baking was done on an iron tripod (croue) over an open fire of ling or gorse 'bons'. The fire had to be fed constantly to provide a slow, but steady heat, which was almost smokeless.

1 lb. plain flour
1 teaspoon salt
1 teaspoon bicarbonate of soda
1 teaspoon cream of tartar
½ pint very sour buttermilk or cream
(fresh milk with a drop of vinegar in it is a reasonable substitute).

Mix the bicarbonate of soda and the cream of tartar with the liquid. Sieve the flour and salt into a bowl and add the liquid. Mix to a soft dough. Turn onto a floured board and knead lightly. Roll out on one side only to about 1½ in. thick. Without turning it over, bake on a hot griddle. Alternatively, bake the cake in a moderate oven for about 40 minutes. Allow to cool before cutting.

Mending nets (Photo: G.B. Cowen) By kind permission of Manx National Heritage

Mutton Hot-Pot

It was said that the three things the old Manx loved above all from an Epicurean point of view were 'skeddan' (herring), 'cowree' (flummery) and 'prinjeig' (haggis).

Prinjeig was made from the stomach of a sheep filled with small pieces of meat, potatoes, onions and groats and boiled for a long time.

It was common to salt down a sheep for food in the winter months. Mutton was used in broths and hot-pots; thin slices of mutton fried in a pan like bacon was known as 'maken'.

In 1660, a side of mutton cost one shilling and sixpence, while geese sold for fourpence each, hens for twopence, eggs cost a penny a dozen and butter was one shilling and two pence a pound.

Neck of mutton
2 onions
1 lb. potatoes
Water to cover
Salt and pepper

Put the mutton in a meat dish, season, and cover with water. Lay the sliced onions and potatoes on top of the meat and season again. Bake in a moderate oven for two to three hours until the potatoes are browned on top. Serve with pickled red cabbage.

Lynague, German

Jugged Hare

1 hare
1 rasher of bacon
1 – 2 oz. dripping
1 ½ pints stock
1 ½ oz. flour
1 onion stuck with 2 cloves
Seasoning
Small bay leaf,
4 peppercorns, tied together in a muslin bag
blade of mace,
1 teaspoon redcurrant jelly
1 glass red wine

Prepared hare, reserving blood, liver, heart and kidneys. Fry the joints and bacon in the fat. When the meat is lightly browned, cover with stock, stir in blended flour, onion, seasoning and bag of herbs. Cover and cook very gently in a moderate oven or on top of the stove until tender - about three hours. Just before serving, remove the onion and herbs, stir in the strained blood, jelly and wine and re-heat without boiling.

Tram in the snow, Ballaglass

How to Pott Hare, Very Good

From a late 18th century recipe book

Take a large Hare, Skin and wash it clean, then put it down in a pot of Boiling water with six onions, a sprig of thyme, some Bayleaves and some whole pepper and a rasher of Bacon. When it is boyled enough, take it up and bone it and mince it, then put it in a marble mortar with four blades or more of mace, broke small. Then pound the Hare to a fine Paste. Take out all strings then put your paste in small potting pots, pressed down hard. Put fresh butter, melted, over them. When cold, cover with paper.

Beef, Leek and Potato Hot-Pot

½ lb. stewing steak
1 lb. leeks
2 lbs. Potatoes

Boil the beef for half an hour, then add the sliced leek and sliced potatoes. Season with salt and pepper. Let simmer on the stove for another hour and a half, or until cooked.

Shore Road, Peel

Salted Liver

Once or twice a year, on most farms, a pig was killed and salted down for use in the months to follow.The head was made into brawn and the fat was made into dripping. A very common breakfast dish was 'crackling' - thin slices of rind fried until crisp and eaten with bread and butter. Salted pig's liver was cut thinly and roasted in front of the fire on a long fork.

Place the liver on a tray with a thick layer of coarse salt over and under it. Turn the liver every day for about eight days, working it well into the brine. Hang to dry in a good draught. It should hang for at least 10 days before cutting.

Jugged Manx Kippers

A quick and easy way to cook kippers, with no greasy pan to wash afterwards!

Cut off the heads and tails from the kippers. Place heads down in a tall heatproof jug. Fill with boiling water and cover. After 6 to 8 minutes, drain well and serve on heated plates with a knob of butter and a wedge of lemon or a sliced tomato.

'Dreem Beary', German. The author's grandfather was born here.

Roast Rabbit

1 rabbit skinned and prepared
Sage and onion stuffing
Bacon fat
Potatoes, carrots and turnips

Clean the skinned rabbit in salted water. Stuff the belly with sage and onion stuffing. Draw the sides together and stitch up. Spoon bacon fat over the rabbit and bake in a moderate oven for about two hours. Serve with potatoes, carrots and turnips.

Sage and Onion Stuffing

4 oz. dry bread
2 large onions
1 tablespoon mashed potato
2 teaspoons dried sage
A knob of margarine
½ teaspoon salt
¼ teaspoon pepper

Pour warm water over the dry bread and leave to soak. Meanwhile, boil the onions until tender and chop them finely. Drain the water off the bread, pressing out as much moisture as possible. Crumble the bread into the chopped onions. Add the mashed potato, margarine and chopped sage and season well with salt and pepper.

Rechabite procession, Peel

Salt Duck

Place the duck on a dish which has been sprinkled liberally with salt. Put a small handful of salt inside the duck and another layer of salt over the bird. Leave for 24 hours.Then wash the bird well and boil slowly for an hour (more if it is not a young bird). Serve with onion sauce. The traditional vegetables to serve with salt duck were boiled kale (or cabbage) and potatoes, mashed together in equal parts.

Onion Sauce

4 onions
2 – 3 tablespoons cornflour
½ pint of milk
½ oz butter
Grated rind of 1 lemon
Salt and pepper

Cover the onions with salted water, boil and simmer for about 10 - 15 minutes or until soft. Drain, but save half a pint of the liquor. Put the cornflour in a basin and blend with two tablespoons of the milk. Mix the remainder of the milk with the onion liquor, add the butter and bring to the boil.Add the boiled liquid to the blended cornflour, stirring briskly. Return the mixture to the pan and re-boil, stirring continuously until it thickens. Stir in the salt, pepper, grated lemon rind and cooked onions.

Church bazaar, Ramsey (Photo: Midwood)

Christmas Bunloaf

The Christmas break must have been a very welcome holiday, for it lasted a full two weeks. During this 'Kegeesh Ommidagh' (Foolish Fortnight) it was forbidden to do any but the most necessary work. On Christmas Eve, homes were decorated with evergreens. Young and old too attended the Oie'll Verrey in the local chapel. It would be getting very late when they made their way home, some stopping off at the public house for a drink or two of 'jough-vie', mulled, spiced ale. The party would continue into the early hours until the big candle had burned down in its socket.

Bunloaf, a sticky fruit loaf made without eggs was traditionally served to visitors at Christmas.

1 ½ lb. plain flour
½ lb. large raisins
½ lb. currants
½ lb. sultanas
½ lb. mixed peel
½ lb. sugar
10 oz. butter or margarine
½ teaspoon mixed spice
½ teaspoon cinnamon
1 tablespoon syrup
2 teaspoons bicarbonate of soda
1 pint buttermilk
(or fresh milk with a drop of vinegar)

Sieve flour and spices into a large bowl and rub in the fat.

The 'Lil Ev'rin'

Add sugar, mixed peel and fruit. Put bicarbonate of soda in a basin and mix smoothly with the milk. Pour into the dry ingredients. Finally, add the syrup and mix thoroughly. Put into a greased and lined baking tin. Bake in a moderate oven for two hours. Or, put in two 1 lb loaf tins and bake in a moderate oven for approximately one hour. When cool, wrap in greaseproof paper.

Thomas Moore, of Port Erin, recalled Christmas Day in his youth when the only means of cooking the bird was in a huge pot-oven hung over the fire.

'The pie was made. As a rule, there was a whole goose along with other things, with a very massive crust on top. Then the fire was made of turf under the pot and a fire placed on top of the lid.'

The Manx equivalent of the Yule Log was the 'Big Peat', but even so, it must have taken a long time for that pie to cook!

Proverb:
Ayns yn Ollick bee mayd gennal,
Tra ta 'n jough goll mygeart,
Tra ta'n chiollagh ooilley sollys,
As yn foaid mooar ooilley kiart.

At the Christmas we'll be merry,
When the ale is flowing round,
When the hearth is all ablaze,
With the big turf in its place.

Snow over North Barrule

Temperatures, Weights and Measures

Quick Conversions - Temperatures

	°F	Electric °C	Gas
Very Slow Oven	250–275	120–140	¼–½
Slow	300–325	150–160	1–2
Moderate	350–375	180–190	3–5
Moderately Hot	375–400	190–200	5–6
Hot	400–425	230–250	6–7
Very Hot	450–475	230–250	8–9

Quick Conversions - Weights

1 lb. is approximately ½ kg.
1 oz. is approximately 30 g.

Quick Conversions - Measures

1 gallon is approximately 4 litres.
1 pint is approximately ½ litre.
1 cup is approximately ½ pint or 10 fluid ounces or 300 millilitres.
1 teacup is approximately ⅓ pint or 7 fluid ounces or 200 millilitres.
1 tablespoon is approximately ⅗ fluid ounce or 15 millilitres.
1 dessertspoon is approximately ⅖ fluid ounce or 10 millilitres.
1 teaspoon is approximately ⅕ fluid ounce or 5 millilitres. (a standard medicine spoon – 5 millilitres).

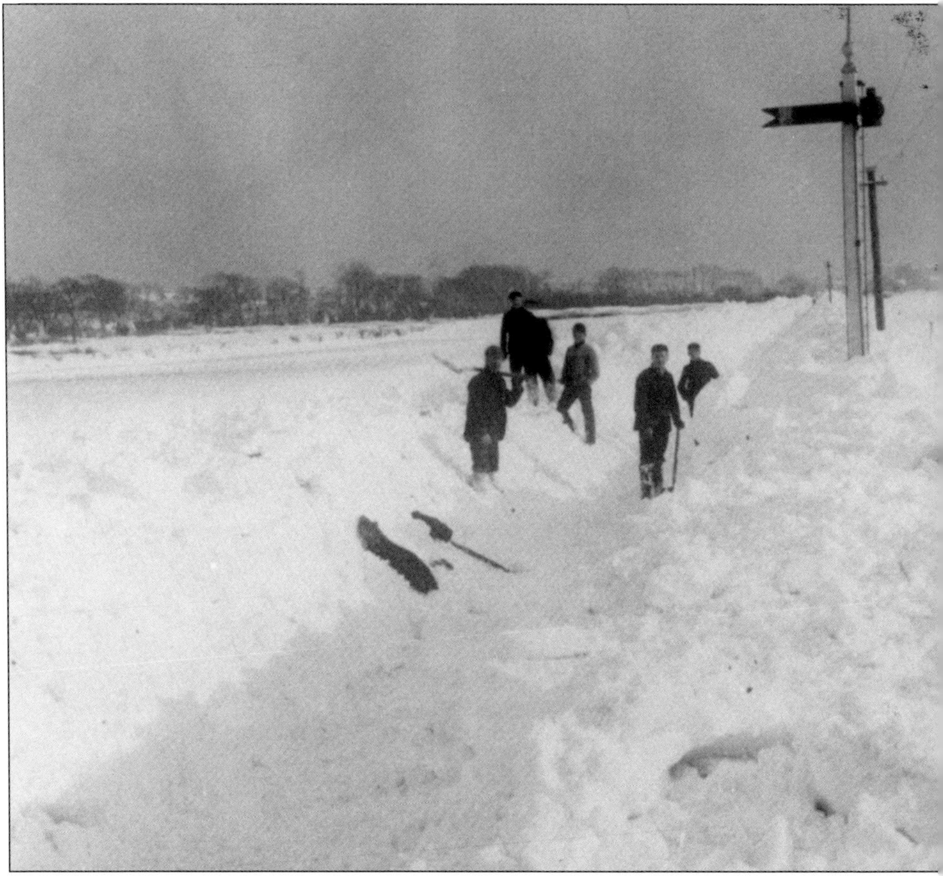

Big Snow

Extracts from Vocabulary of the Anglo-Manx Dialect compiled by A.W. Moore (1924)

ATE, AIT, eat
You'll praise the mait
Before you ait,
And when it's ett
You'll sthreight forget. (Said to an ingrate.)

BLITHE-MEAT, the meal prepared for visitors at the birth of a child. This term has gone out of use and has been replaced by the phrase 'There's bread and cheese going'.
Small pieces of bread and cheese called blithe-meat.

BOB-Y-LANE, BOBLANE, sea-bobs, an edible sea tang, *Alaria esculeata.*
Children eat the 'rib' of the Boblane, and the 'bob' of pendants attached to its lower end, but the tough footstalk known as sleepy head by which it adheres to the rock is seldom eaten as it 'cribs' the mouth.

BRAGHTAN, a griddle-cake sandwiched with cheese, or meat, or herring, &c; a sandwich; anything flattened.
Put a braghtan in thee pocket.
Thou've sat on me hat and made a braghtan of it.

BROISH, broken pieces of cake soaked in broth or milk. 'Broish feill', bread soaked in gravy. 'Broish vainney', milk broish. 'Broish bithag', thick cream broish. 'Broish geir', buttermilk broish. 'Broish mulish', new milk broish. 'Broish phidher', pea soup.

BROOILLAGH, crumbs, fragments.
These priddas is all gone to brooillagh.

COWREE, sowens, fiummery. Cowree and Scouse were two favourite dishes ; the former was made from the inner husk of oats, the latter was a kind of meat stew.
And cowree, juice of oatmeal's husky seed
That on this mountain banquet takes the lead.

CRAME, 'cream'.
As sweet as sugar and as soft as crame.
What's yer name?
Butther an' crame.
Who give ye that name?
My Aunty Jane. (Children's rhyme.)

DOLLY, to work up, whisk up.
She'll dolly anything up for dinner for them, shake flour over the coul' taters from the day before and curl them up on the pan and call them some Frinch name - aw, she'll dolly any mortal ha'porth for the lodgers' dinner.

CROPPEE, drinking-horn.
That Croppee or lairk has been in our family for six generations - handed on from father to son 'for luck'.

BREWING-PAN
A gossip is said to go about like a brewing-pan. One brewing-pan, or kettle, once served for a whole neighbourhood and was passed on from landowner to landowner. In some instances it was parish property. The light beer called 'jough' (Manx = drink) thus made was for the most part brewed by each family for its own use.

FITTY [fiti], literally something 'fit' to eat, applied to an edible shore crab.
Bhoys-y-bhoys, I've found a fitty!

FUMBYREE [fùmbari] (Manx), 'flummery', furmity, hulled barley or wheat boiled in milk and seasoned with sugar and spice.
Sollaghan and owree,
Fumbyree and cowree,
Pease porridge hot,
Pease porridge coul',
Pease porridge in the pot
Nine days oul'. (Children's rhyme.)

GRAMMASY, GRUMASY, (Manx *greim* 'morsel', and *mestey,* 'mixture'; cf. Irish *gramaisc,* and Scottish Gaelic, *gramasg),* refuse of food, rubbish, trash; broken victuals.
Aw, no, I wudn like to go to France at all ; they're sayin you'll get nothin to eat there but gramasies.
There was a plate on the floor full of grumasy for the dog.
Nothin lef' on the table for supper for me but a lot of grumasy.

HOMPS, HOMS, grab.
'Ta homs cairagh echey' (he has a right grab), ie. he has made a good meal. 'Ny bee homsal cha tappee' (do not be grabbing so quick), ie. do not eat so ravenously. When used in speaking Anglo-Manx it becomes capable of somewhat eccentric varieties of meaning. Of a covetous person it is said that 'he is always on for a homps', ie. ready for a grab; and of fish that 'they made a homps at the bait'. But a fisherman on returning home at dinner-time will say, 'Is me homps (food) ready?'

JEETRYM-JEES (Manx: jeetdrym jeeas), mare's-tail, Hippuris vulgaris.
Some is callin jeetrym-jees mare's tails, and others is callin it hoss-tails. Take lus-y-jeetdrym-jeeas (herb mare's-tail) and boil it, and sup the water, and it'll soon aise yer bowels (bowels).

JENNY-NETTLE, JINNY-NETTLE, stinging-nettle; also a name for jelly-fish.
They're gatherin jinny nettles to make beer. Some people like a birro jinny nettle in the Sunday's broth.

JOCKEY-BAR, the broad, flat top-bar of a kitchen grate.
The kettle was singing on the jockey-bar. Put the kettle sittin on the jockey.

JOUGH, ale.
'Jough-yn-Ollick', or 'Jough y Nollick'. Manx: lit. 'drink of the Christmas', 'Christmas beer'
They used to be brewin a bettermos' surt of ale fur joughy-Nollick.

KITCHEN, **KYTSHEN**, anything eaten as a relish with bread, potatoes, or other plain fare.
Give me a bit o' kitchen.
Navar nothin at them for kytshen but herrin.
Always two or three sorts of kytshen goin on the table.

KNOBS, **NOBS**, sweetmeats made of toffee in small irregular shapes.
His pockets stuffed with knobs to be givin to the youngsters.

MOLLAG [molag] (Manx), an inflated sheepskin tarred and used as a buoy to float herring nets.
He come home about half an hour ago as full as a mollag, ie. as full of drink as a mollag is full of wind.

PRIDDA, **PRIDDHA, PRIDDHAR**, 'potato'.
Hafe a pridda, hafe an egg,
Tha's a feed for Jinny veg.
Let me see you stir afoot till them priddhas is peelt!
Yandher one is that fine-spoken she can't say 'pridda'.
Well of all the names tha's goin on the surts o' priddas! – there's Kemps and Rocks and Flour-balls-and Belldhrums and Blues and Red-pennies-and Bill Johns and Paddy Kraaylls and Magna-bonas (Magnum bonum), and hardly the one o' them'll come up to the Champions and the Mona's Prides.

PRINJEIG, paunch, haggis.
A gool chain across his prinjeig.
There's a big prinjeig at that fellow, ie. he is very consequential.
We had a sheep's prinjeig for dinner, haggidge ye know.

PURT, **PHURT,** port, harbour. Among the jocular names for a cooked herring are 'Purt Iern (Port Erin) beef', 'Purtle-Moirrey (Port St. Mary) steak', and 'Purt-ny.hinshey (Peel) duck'. 'Purt-na-marnee' (Manx: Purt ny Manninee, 'Port of the Manxmen'), a name for Peel: – She tuk the cart to Purt-na-marnee to gerr her stock of herrin.

PIECE, a slice of bread.
Atin pieces all the day. Them childher is doin nothin but piecin and stuffin their bellies.

Piece upon piece upon the trencher, Piece upon the trencher,
Cut it small, eat it all,
Very fine food for winter.
(Two girls with clasped hands sing the rhyme while see-sawing each other on heels and toes.)

PUNCH-MULLAG (Manx: mullag, 'a cask'), cask punch, liquor obtained by filling the emptied spirit casks with boiling water. *He got dhrunk on punch mullag. This rum is no sthronger till punchmollag,*

PURK, 'pork'.
Sally Magaary's pig is dead, We'll have purk and oaten bread.
(Said by children on seeing a pig being killed.)
I've heard in Glen Rushen, in my young days: Fin MacCooley's pig is dead, We'll get purk and oaten bread.

ROAGAN, **RAUGAN**, (Manx: shlig-roagan), the large scollop, Pecten maximus. It is about six inches in diameter. One of its shells is flat and is called the 'plate', the other is deeply rounded, and is called the 'basin'. Both served in old times as crockery. The saucer-like shell when filled with cod oil was used as a lamp, a peeled rush or a strip of rag serving as wick. *Many is the time I seen a roagan put on the top of a jug and doin for a lamp.*
When we were childher we used to be borin holes in raugans and puttin sthrings through, and makin a pair of scales and weighin sand in them pitendin we were sellin shop (keeping shop).

SAUCY, fastidious.
It's a middlin saucy body that wudn ate it. I'm saucy-

hungry to night, i. e. not hungry enough to eat plain food, but requiring the palate to be tempted.

SCAVEEN, morsel.
He don't want a scaveen to ate on the day.

SKEDHAN, SKADDHIN, SCADHAN, (Manx: skeddan), herring.
Nothin goin for dinner only 'praasyn as skeddan' (priddas and herrin).
Scaddhan boys, a name for Peel men: - He was jus' a scadhan boy from the fag-end of creation, the las' place God made, and that's Peel.

SKILLAGALEE, thin oatmeal, porridge, gruel.
Haven't ye enough meal in the house? This porridge is proper skillagalee. She's a skillagalee of a craythur.
Skillagalee
At half past three,
A little more
At half past four.
(Said in derision to one who has been 'put in the Castle' and fed on prison fare.)

SKIM-BLUE, skimmed milk.
The boys would be goin roun' sellin skimmilk urrov kegs that was slung on each side of a donkey - and they would be shoutin,
Milk he-aw! (here) Skim blue,
Chalk and water, Good milk too!

SKIMMILKY, like skimmed milk.
Some surt of a kiss very skimmilky, very could. Tha's like skimmilk afther craem!

SNIPER, a dram of spirits, a morning drink. *He mus' be havin a sniper of a mornin.*

SAMSON, a beverage made of treacle and hops; it was considered to be a great strengthener.
I remember Uncle sending to the village a large jar to be filled with 'Samson' for a drink for the people working in the harvest field.